Portholme Mead

History, Management and Wildlife

by Dr J Patrick Doody, Brampton

Other books by Dr J Patrick Doody

Brampton Walks for the Millennium - ISBN 1 902869 17 6
Brampton Parish lanscape & natural history - ISBN 1 902869 21 4

Published & Printed by Just Print IT! Publications
59 The Whaddons, Huntingdon, Cambs. PE29 1NW
Tel: 01480 450880
www.just-printit.com

ISBN 1 902869 28 1

First Edition

By Dr J Patrick Doody

Brampton

July 2006

This is the third in a series of booklets on Brampton Parish, its landscape and wildlife. It describes the land-use history and management of Portholme Meadow and its influence on the landscape and wildlife we see today. Other booklets in the series are:

- *"Brampton Walks for the Millennium"*, describes a number of walks and features of interest in the Parish;
- *"Brampton Parish landscape and natural history"*, describes the history from the Ice-age to the present day and its influence on the landscape.

These are available from the author price £2.99 plus 50p postage. Email pat.doody@ntlworld.com or send a cheque to 5 Green Lane, Brampton, Huntingdon, Cambs., PE28 4RE.

Dedication: Derek Wells, late of Hilton, a friend and colleague to whom I owe a great deal.

*I*ntroduction. Portholme Meadow is a large, unenclosed river flood plain meadow, bordered on two sides by the River Great Ouse in the Parish of Brampton, in Cambridgeshire. It is mostly at or below the OS 10 metre contour and is regularly flooded in winter. It has a rich history of human use as a racecourse, an airfield and is managed for hay and sheep and cattle grazing. It supports a rich flora and is a haven for a number of less common breeding birds in summer (e.g. corn bunting and skylark) now absent from much of the more intensively farmed Cambridgeshire landscape. It also supports large populations of ducks, waders and gulls when flooded in winter. It is designated as a Site of Special Scientific Interest and is recognised internationally as a Special Area of Conservation under the European Union 'Habitats' Directive.

*L*ocation. Saxton's map of Huntingdon clearly shows the route of the River Great Ouse and the location of "Port Med". Although the river flows are controlled today by the Environment Agency, its course remains largely the same as it was in 1607 (see the map below). When it reaches Earith in the east, the work of Cornelius Vermuyden and others straightened the river to facilitate drainage of the surrounding 'fen' land. This work, carried out in stages from 1634, was finally completed in 1652. This almost certainly cut off the influence of the tide to the Ouse river above Earith bridge.

*G*eology. Portholme Meadow lies over a bed of calcareous Oxford Clay. This was deposited some 160 million years ago during the Jurassic Period (the Age of the Dinosaurs). This layer can be up to 70 m thick in places. Covering this are more recent deposits. The last, and one of the most extensive glaciations, the Anglian Glaciation stretched as far south as London. Lasting from about 500,000 to 12,000 years ago, the ice was up to 1,000 metres thick in the north . As the ice melted for the last time, sand and gravel was washed into the river valleys. This created the deep bed of gravel and mixed deposits which underlie the meadow.

*S*oils. The meadow is bordered by the River Great Ouse to the south and east, Alcolnbury Brook to the north, and by a stream running along its western boundary. These features are clearly seen on Blome's map of 1673, below.

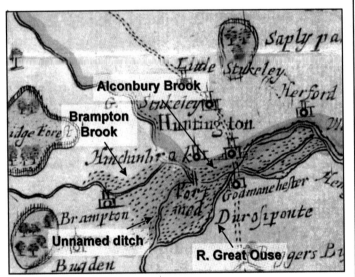

Top soil: to 0.3 m

Clayey alluvium to 0.6/0.7 m

"Upper" Terrace Deposits: Clay with sand and fine gravel to 0.9/1.3 m

"Lower" Terrace Deposits: Gravel

to 4.8 m

Oxford Clay up to 70 m

*M*aps that predate the draining of the fens, such as Blaue's map of East Anglia (dated 1643), show 'fen' stretching right up into the river valleys. Given that the canalised Ouse is still tidal at Earith, it seems likely that this stretched to, and included, Portholme. The combination of tidal movement and freshwater runoff probably resulted in the land being flooded for much of the time in winter. Hence, although early settlements occurred in the river valleys, places like Portholme were probably only used in the summer months.

arly settlement. Neolithic people settled in the river valleys such as the Great Ouse. Here the underlying gravel helped to create well-drained soils, at least in comparison to the heavily wooded clays that surrounded them. Neolithic remains have been found at several sites around Portholme (Archaeology sites in Huntingdon, source The Huntingdonshire Forum web site). There is no information about the use of the site at this time, although it seems likely at Huntingdon the river provided access to the sea, even though it was 60 km away.

ark Ages to 1066. It was in the period following the invasion of the Vikings, and Huntingdon becoming a Saxon borough, that a complicated channel system between Portholme Meadow and Godmanchester was created. This provided a head of water for a succession of water mills. So control of the water system in and around Portholme appears to have a very early origin. There is no reference to Portholme in the Doomsday Book though it does mention 2 mills in Brampton and 3 in, Godmanchester.

istorical management. The first reference to the management of Portholme is that of King John, who in 1212 granted a charter of Common Rights. This charter prevented the area being divided, developed or enclosed and also imposed strict rules to its use. For example, animals were not allowed onto the ground until "Stocking Day" the 13th May, when the herds boy of each common patrolled the streets at 4.00 am blowing a cow's horn. This suggests grazing in the summer rather than winter as occurs today. Things probably changed following the drainage of the fens in the mid 1600s with the control of the river at Earith.

epys, the famous diarist, lived for some time in Brampton. Four entries in his diary give an indication of the management at that time:

1. 14th July 1661. *(Lord's day).* ".. in the evening my father and I walked round Portholme and viewed all the fields, which was very pleasant.
2. 13th October 1662. "... and with my father took a melancholy walk to Portholme, seeing the country-maids milking their cows there, they being there now at grass, and to see with what mirth they come all home together in pomp with their milk, and sometimes they have musique go before them."
3. 26th May 1664. "...thence to Sir R. Bernard, and there received ...in part of Piggot's L209 due to us, which L40 he pays for 7 roods of meadow in Portholme."
4. 24th May 1668. "...while I to my father, poor man, and walked with him up and down the house-it raining a little, and the waters all over Portholme and the meadows, so as no pleasure abroad."

looding in autumn and spring, grazing in winter and hay in July seem to be the order of the day. Pepys, or at least his father, appears to have some Commoner Rights. Receiving money for "7 roods of meadow", although it is not clear if this was for hay or from grazing rights. Note: Sir Rob' Bernard is one of the major 'owners' of part of several "Doles" on Portholme as shown on the Enclosure Survey of 1772. Today, although several cottages in Brampton Village may still have rights attached their deeds, these are no longer exercised.

*R**ace days at Portholme.* Some of the earliest records of racing, as we know it, were arranged at Huntingdon from 1607, although these may have been near Sapley. The first edition of the Racing Calendar in 1773 details flat races run on Portholme, and it appears racing was already well established by then. Horace Walpole, writing in 1760, described the Huntingdon races as more than a little local affair. They ranked with the Derby as one of the nation's fashionable events of the year. It appears that the meetings went from strength to strength and by 1824 were probably as important as any in England. Flat racing under jockey club rules took place here for more than 200 years, until it apparently went downhill. It last appeared in the racing calendar in 1896, due to lack of interest.

*P*ortholme's circuit was two miles in circumference and is clearly shown on several maps (see for example OS maps of **1835 and 1890/92**). The races began on the first Tuesday in August each year and continued for 3 days. The course was well endowed with grandstands, footbridges (see picture by Weell, which shows a grandstand 'on stilts'). Other facilities for supplementary activities included fairgrounds, cockfighting, boxing etc.

"View of GODMANCHESTER and Huntingdon Race Ground", Portholme from a picture (undated) by Geo Weell, by kind permission, the Norris Museum, St Ives.

*H*orses and cattle can be seen grazing in the picture, which if the painting is from a scene in August would be entirely in keeping with the prescribed management of the site. For a detailed description of the development of racing in Huntingdon see:

Hudson, N., 1985. *Catherine the Great to Wordsworth - 100 Years of Huntingdon Steeplechasing*. Huntingdon Steeplechases Ltd., Cambridge.

A*viators.* At the beginning of the 20th Century, Portholme became a mecca for early attempts at flight, its flat terrain being perfect for take off and landing. So much so that in 1910, only one year after Bleriot's cross-channel flight, it was proposed that Portholme be established as "an aviation course" (see map below). The Portholme Aviation Company made a small number of aeroplanes but by 1912 went out of business. However, despite a brief respite in the Great War, when the Admiralty ordered several sea planes, these were not a success. For further information see:

Buist, H.M., 1992. *Huntingdon the Aviation Centre.* Huntingdon Local History Society.

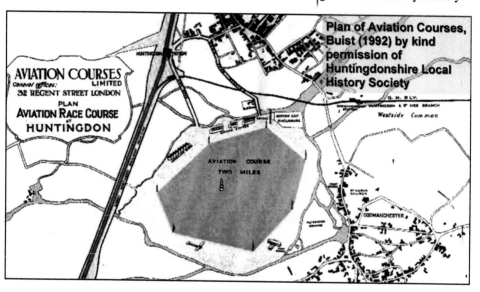

R*oyal Flying Corps training station.* In the years of the Great War and up until the early 1930s Portholme was used by the Royal Flying Corps (see opposite). At one time it was also proposed that the site become an airport. Thankfully, the periodic flooding, so important to the maintenance of the nature conservation interest, made it less than suitable for this activity.

Bleriot monoplane, on Portholme

*E*nclosure Acts. Portholme was common land and several houses in Brampton held rights to graze animals. When the land surveys for the enclosure acts took place in Brampton Parish in 1772, Portholme was dealt with as a separate entity. The enclosure map (see below) shows the apportionment of the land as Freehold, Copyhold and Allotment. The last can be very large with several assigned to the same person (one such being Sir Robert Bernard's "First Allotment"; "First Allotment Freehold"; "Fourth Allotment Copyhold" etc. who after Lord Sandwich was the largest beneficiary).

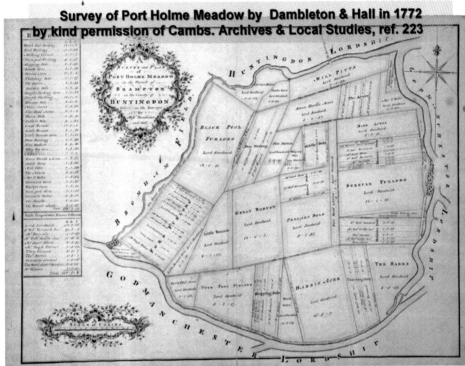

Survey of Port Holme Meadow by Dambleton & Hall in 1772 by kind permission of Cambs. Archives & Local Studies, ref. 223

*B*rampton Enclosure Extracts 1772. These first refer to stints for Port Holme then: "….subject nevertheless to the rules orders and directions hereinafter mentioned that is to say that the said meadow called Port Holme shall be opened for cows and horses from the first day of Sept and shut on the 20 Nov in every year and that it shall not be lawful for any commoners or occupiers of right of common upon the same meadow and after the said 20 Nov till the said 1 Sept to turn feed or depasture any cows or horses thereafter. And also that the said meadow shall be opened to sheep on the 21 November in every year and shut on the 1 February both inclusive and that it shall not be lawful for any of the owners or occupiers of common rights upon the sd meadow from and after the sd 1 Feb till the sd 21 Nov to turn feed or depasture any sheep thereon."

*O*wnership. Today, most of the site is owned by the London Angling Society who receive the proceeds of the sale of hay and aftermath grazing. A small portion of the meadow totalling about 4 acres, viz. Milking Corner (2 acres within Ford Furlong), Haddon Dole (5 roods) and Thacking Dole (3 roods), is owned by the Thomas Miller Charity. In his will of 1681, Thomas Miller left to "the Town of Brampton" three parcels of land on Portholme (shown on the map below) the rent from which should be used as follows:

- ten shillings (50p) to be paid to the Minister of the Parish every year for preaching a sermon on New Year's Day;
- the rest to be distributed to the poor in Easter Week.

*R*ent. Sale of hay from Portholme realises on average, about £90 per annum. The Charity derives the bulk of its money from interest on investments. The Parish Council is responsible for appointing 2 of the three Trustees, each serving for 4 years. The Rector of Brampton Parish Church is an ex-officio trustee. Information supplied by D.L. Hellary, Clerk and Trustee.

Copy of the "Site Plan" for the "Mowing Grass Sale & Aftermath Grazing" for 2006 . Note the layout is exactly the same as in 1772!

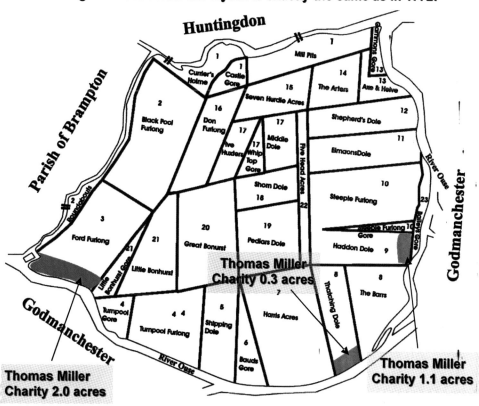

*M*anagement. The present management of Portholme meadow can be traced at least as far back as the enclosure Acts of the late 1700s. However, it seems likely that the basis of the management structure was in place long before then. This is perhaps the most important aspect of this site and closely links traditional agricultural use with the conservation of the features for which the site is identified at national and European levels. The fact that the site has not been subject to intensive agricultural use, including ploughing and the extensive application of artificial fertilizers, has allowed a number of herbs, lost from other permanent but 'improved' grassland, to survive. The pattern of management (detailed on the previous page), described in 1772, was probably largely a continuation of a much older pattern. The hay crop and aftermath grazing are sold each year at auction by (Alexanders Auctioneers, Huntingdon) on or around the 15th June.

*L*ots are marked out by 'main roadways' cut prior to the sale and in accordance with the pattern shown on the previous page. Up until recently (c 1980) they were identified by 'lining up' features such as church spires and locating depressions in the ground at the corners of the lots. Today, concrete slabs and use of a Global Positioning System do the same job.

Local farmer John Sewell marking out the 'roadways', June 2006

*C*onditions of sale. All the lots are to be "mown by the 31st July and carted off by the 8th August next under penalty of 50p per acre for each day that it remains uncut or uncleared." "The purchasers shall not be allowed to depasture horses or any livestock on any of the lots." The aftermath winter grazing is also sold and the grazing levels set at:

- 281 cattle from the 1st September to the 20th November;
- 334 sheep from the 21st November to the 28th February.

$\mathcal{F}$ ertilisers or herbicides are not allowed. These are restrictions imposed by Natural England (formerly English Nature), the agency responsible for ensuring the maintenance of the nature conservation value of the site. They have also imposed a restriction on the date when the hay is cut, which has been put back two weeks to the 1st July. Today cattle and sheep are often seen on the site together. In 2005 and 2006 the sheep were joined by a unusual visitor, a red deer, see below!

$\mathcal{H}$ ay values vary considerably from year to year (see table below). Note some of the smaller acreages have been omitted. This is partly related to the time of year when flooding occurs and the number of days of inundation. The general tailing off of values observed since 1991, appears to be related to the increase of dock (*Rumex acetosa*). Some of the highest prices paid are for the botanically richer areas.

Lot number		Area	Price £ / acre			
	Lot Name	(acres)	1991	1994	1998	2005
1	Mill Pits; Castle Gore; Curriers Holme	11.2.0	14	15	14	22
2	Blackpool Furlong; The Roundabouts & Swathes	25.2.15	30	29	10	18
3	Ford Furlong	17.0.0	24	30	14	18
4	Turnpool Gore; Turnpool Furlong	13.0.0	28	32	14	18
5	Shipping Dole	10.0.0	24	30	12	18
7	Harris Acres	21.0.0	30	42	18	22
8	Thatching|Dole; The Barrs	17.0.0	16	42	6	15
9	Haddon Dole	9.3.0	24	45	10	14
10	Steeple Furlong	19.2.0	46	41	10	18
11	Elmons Dole	10.0.0	42	39	16	14
12	Shepherds Dole	9.0.0	38	29	10	15
15	Seven Acres Hurdle	7.0.0	28	21	10	4
16	Dam Furlong	9.2.0	38	35	10	16
17	Five Huxters; Whip Top Gore; Middle Dole	13.0.0	30	20	7	7
19	Pedlars Dole	10.0.0	32	32	25	22
20	Great Bonurst	15.0.0	42	45	30	22
21	Little Bonurst; Little Bonurst Gore	12.0.0	46	47	18	22
25	Grazing aftermath	255.0.0	600	600	600	380

The red deer on Portholme, November 2005

*F*looding is important to the productivity of the meadow and the maintenance of the rich grassland communities. In the absence of artificial fertiliser applications, which are not allowed, periodic flooding is part of the management cycle, bringing much needed nutrients into the site. The maintenance of the river flow is the responsibility of the Environment Agency. The River Great Ouse catchment is covered by the extensive 3,000 km^2 Upper Ouse and Bedford Ouse, Abstraction Management Strategy. The strategy aims to manage abstraction in order to meet the reasonable needs of abstractors, while leaving enough water in the environment to conserve aquatic habitats, and for other water users.

Portholme from Godmanchester lock, this low-lying area can remain waterlogged for weeks at a time, February 2007

*W*inter flooding is the norm. Pepys refers to Portholme being flooded in May 1668. This seems to be unusually late. Bank-full data from the Environment Agency show the pattern of inundation. Periods when the site is partly flooded for a few days occur most often. More extreme events are less frequent, with the winters of 2000/1 and 2003/4 having particularly prolonged periods of inundation. Compare this with the winter of 2001/2 which was particularly dry. Not all events result in the complete coverage of the site. Although in 2003/4 Alconbury Brook completely disappeared for several days (see the picture opposite).

*S*pring appears to have been the most common period when flooding occurred in the past. In recent years (1993 onwards) anecdotal information, from the former English Nature Conservation Officers, suggests that there has been an increase in autumn flooding, notably in 2000/1. Coupled with a tendency for the duration of flooding to increase, this has led to adverse changes taking place in the vegetation. Longer periods of inundation can cause die-back in flood-sensitive species. Additional nutrients can favour coarser grasses and herbs, at the expense of some of the less common species.

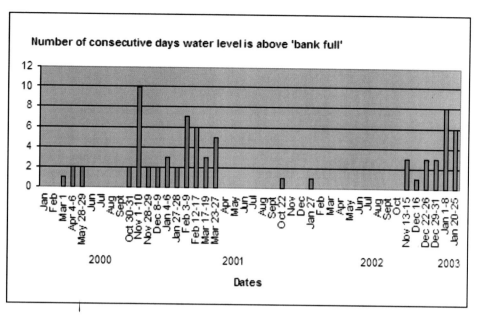

Number of consecutive days water level is above 'bank full'

Dates

2000   2001   2002   2003

D o c k ,
(*R u m e x
acetosa),*
in particular, seems to
have responded to the
long period of
flooding in 2000/1.
This resulted in it
becoming visually
dominant over much
of the north eastern
part of the site. (see
picture opposite). The
picture below shows
the extent of flooding
in January 2003.

Portholme completely flooded in 2003/4

V *egetation of lowland hay meadows*. Pepys, in a diary entry, refers to Portholme as being "*the largest and most flowery spot the sun ever beheld*". Whilst this may be something of an exaggeration nowadays, it is an internationally important site as an example of a 'lowland hay meadow', formally designated by English Nature as a Site of Special Scientific interest. This community is characterised by species-rich swards containing frequent red fescue *Festuca rubra*, crested dog's-tail *Cynosurus cristatus*, meadow foxtail *Alopecurus pratensis*, great burnet *Sanguisorba officinalis*, meadowsweet *Filipendula ulmaria* and meadow buttercup *Ranunculus acris*. It also provides the main habitat in the UK for fritillary *Fritillaria meleagris*. It is one of the types included in the "Natural and semi-natural grassland formations" section of the habitats included for selection under the European Union Habitats Directive. It corresponds to National Vegetation Classification type, Mesotrophic Grasslands (**MG4**) - *Alopecurus pratensis – Sanguisorba officinalis* grassland.

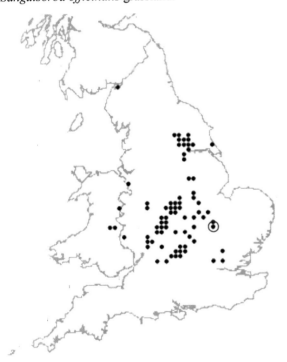

D *istribution* of the vegetation type is restricted in the UK . It occurs almost entirely in central and southern England, with a few scattered sites along the Welsh borders (see map opposite). It is thought to cover less than 1,500 ha, surviving in scattered and mostly small sites. Particularly important concentrations occur in the valley of the River Thames and its tributaries, and in the Vale of York rivers, especially the Derwent.

S *SSI*. The site has a high wildlife value. It is designated under Section 28 of the Wildlife and Countryside Act 1981 as a Site of Special Scientific Interest (SSSI). Natural England (formerly English Nature, the statutory nature conservation body for England) is responsible for ensuring these interests are protected in the light of changes in water management affecting flooding, pollution and eutrophication, as well as threats from developments such as gravel extraction and road building.

*E*uropean Habitats Directive. Portholme Meadow is one of only 5 sites identified as being of international importance for this vegetation type. In 1992 the European Community adopted *Council Directive 92/43/EEC on the conservation of natural habitats and of wild fauna and flora*, known as the Habitats Directives. The Directive obligations relate to the selection, designation and protection of a series of sites, called Special Areas of Conservation (SACs). Portholme is such a site and contributes to a European network of important high-quality. The others are shown on the map opposite. With an area of 104 ha the meadow represents 7% of the total UK resource.

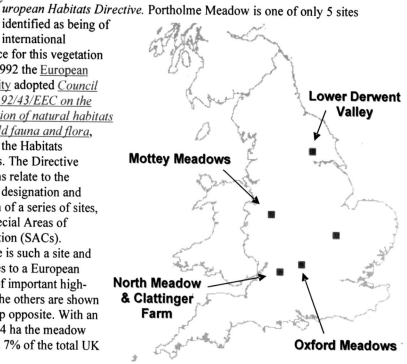

Lower Derwent Valley

Mottey Meadows

North Meadow & Clattinger Farm

Oxford Meadows

Meadow cranesbill and lady's bedstraw, in a herb-rich grassland sward

*P*lants. In addition to the typical, but locally distributed, meadow plants, there are two rare species. The first, narrow-leaved water dropwort (*Oenanthe silaifolia*), is a rather non-descript plant only discovered in 1997 . The second, fritillary (*Fritillaria meleagris*) is an attractive plant first recorded in 1926. The population of this species has risen considerably in recent years, as shown by the increase in flowering spikes in the graph below. Although this is difficult to explain, the life cycle is well adapted to the traditional management regime of Portholme. Seeds are usually produced well before the hay-cut and by this time the plant has died back to an underground bulb.

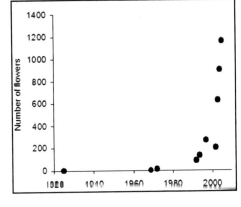

*T*he colony is located at the edge of the lowest part of the site, which remains flooded longer than the rest of the area. Although it does occur in the higher and drier parts of the site it appears to prefer the areas of the meadow that are intermittently flooded. Widespread in England and Wales the plant is now lost from about two thirds of its original sites. Portholme is the only site for the species in the old county of Huntingdonshire.

Fritillaries flowering on Portholme, April 2004

*A*nimals. Portholme is an important site for a number of bird species. Notable amongst these is a small, but thriving population of breeding corn bunting. This species has been displaced from many of the more intensively farmed areas of Cambridgeshire. It can be seen and heard singing (a call that sounds like jangling keys), on the pylons and wires in the centre of the site. Other species that may be encountered at any time of the year, but especially in autumn and spring include: pied wagtails; goldfinches feeding on the abundant hardheads (*Centaurea nigra*); meadow pipits and skylarks.

*W*inter flooding also attracts waders, ducks and gulls. Northern lapwing, golden plover, wigeon and black-headed gulls are sometimes measured in their thousands. Other less common species also appear on the site to take advantage of the rich feeding, including the black-tailed godwit. In January 2007 the following were noted on two visits to the site on the 11th when it was partially flooded.

European Golden Plover	3-4,000+
Northern Lapwing	2,000+
Black-headed Gull	3,000+
Eurasian Wigeon	2,000+
Black-tailed Godwit	250

*F*ieldfares and redwings, winter visitors nesting in Scandinavia, also feed on invertebrates brought to the surface when water levels are near the surface, but not flooded. The species, in the same family as the song thrush, appear in flocks of several hundred. They use Portholme as one of many fuelling stops prior to their northward migration in early Spring.

Golden plovers and lapwings on Portholme, January 2007

Very little information is available for other animals. Several rare invertebrates, include three rare flies and a rare dragonfly. Occasionally, uncommon butterflies such as the clouded yellow can be seen flying over the site and the Horsefly is plentiful!

Yellow-rattle (*Rhinanthus minor*) a semi-parasitic annual of meadows

cknowledgements. My thanks to Kevin Walker, Susan Smith and Bridget Smith, who have given freely of their time and information, and the Environment Agency for details of recent flooding events. Thanks also to the staff from the Cambs. Archives & Local Studies office, Huntingdon and the Norris Museum for their help in identifying the 1772 map and the early picture of the race course. Proceeds from this and the previous 'walks' and 'history' publications will go to the Bedfordshire, Cambridgeshire, Huntingdonshire, Northamptonshire and Peterborough Wildlife Trust, Huntingdon Area Group.

Plant Species List

Latin Name	English name
Achillea millefolium	Yarrow
Achillea ptarmica	Sneezewort
Agrostis stolonifera	Creeping Bent
Alopecurus geniculatus	Marsh Foxtail
Alopecurus pratensis	Meadow Foxtail
Angelica sylvestris	Wild Angelica
Anthoxanthum odoratum	Sweet Vernal-grass
Anthriscus sylvestris	Cow Parsley
Arrhenatherum elatius	False Oat-grass
Atriplex patula	Common Orache
Bellis perennis	Daisy
Berula erecta	Lesser Water-parsnip
Bidens tripartita	Trifid Bur-marigold
Bolboschoenus maritimus	Sea Club Rush
Butomus umbellatus	Flowering Rush
Bromus commutatus	Meadow Brome
Bromus hordeaceus	Soft-brome
Caltha palustris	Marsh Marigold
Calystegia sepium	Hedge Bindweed
Capsella bursa-pastoris	Shepherd's-purse
Cardamine pratensis	Cuckooflower
Carex acuta	Slender Tufted-sedge
Carex disticha	Brown Sedge
Carex hirta	Hairy Sedge
Carex remota	Remote Sedge
Carex riparia	Greater Pond-sedge
Centaurea nigra	Common Knapweed
Cerastium fontanum	Common Mouse-ear
Cirsium arvense	Creeping Thistle
Conopodium majus	Pignut
Cynosurus cristatus	Crested Dog's-tail
Dactylis glomerata	Cock's-foot
Dactylorhiza incarnata	Early Marsh Orchid
Deschampsia cespitosa	Tufted Hair-grass
Eleocharis palustris	Common Spike-rush
Elytrigia repens	Common Couch
Epilobium hirsutum	Great Willowherb
Festuca pratensis	Meadow Fescue
Festuca rubra	Red Fescue
Filipendula ulmaria	Meadowsweet
Filipendula vulgaris	Dropwort
Fritillaria meleagris	Fritillary

Latin Name	English name
Galium palustre	Common Marsh-bedstraw
Galium verum	Lady's Bedstraw
Geranium pratense	Meadow Crane's-bill
Geranium pusillum	Small-flowered Crane's-bill
Glyceria maxima	Reed Sweet-grass
Heracleum sphondylium	Hogweed
Holcus lanatus	Yorkshire-fog
Hordeum secalinum	Meadow Barley
Iris pseudacorus	Yellow Iris
Juncus acutiflorus	Sharp-flowered Rush
Lathyrus pratensis	Meadow Vetchling
Lepidium campestre	Field Pepperwort
Leucanthemum vulgare	Oxeye Daisy
Lolium perenne	Perennial Rye-grass
Lotus corniculatus	Common Bird's-foot-trefoil
Luzula campestris	Field Woodrush
Lychnis flos-cuculi	Ragged-Robin
Lysimachia nummularia	Creeping-Jenny
Lysimachia vulgaris	Yellow Loosestrife
Matricaria discoidea	Pineappleweed
Matricaria recutita	Scented Mayweed
Melilotus albus	White Melilot
Myosotis laxa	Tufted Forget-me-not
Myosotis scorpioides	Water Forget-me-not
Oenanthe crocata	Hemlock Water-dropwort
Oenanthe fistulosa	Tubular Water-dropwort
Oenanthe silaifolia	Narrow-leaved Water-dropwort
Persicaria amphibia	Amphibious Bistort
Phalaris arundinacea	Reed Canary-grass
Phleum bertolonii	Lesser Car's-tail
Phleum pratense agg.	Timothy agg.
Plantago lanceolata	Ribwort Plantain
Plantago major	Greater Plantain
Plantago media	Hoary Plantain
Poa annua	Annual Meadow-grass
Poa trivialis	Rough Meadow-grass
Potentilla anserina	Silverweed
Potentilla reptans	Creeping Cinquefoil
Ranunculus acris	Meadow Buttercup
Ranunculus bulbosus	Bulbous Buttercup
Ranunculus repens	Creeping Buttercup
Rhinanthus minor	Yellow-rattle
Rorippa amphibia	Great Yellow-cress

Latin Name	English name
Rorippa palustris	Marsh Yellow-cress
Rorippa sylvestris	Creeping Yellow-cress
Rumex acetosa	Common Sorrel
Rumex acetosella	Sheep's Sorrel
Rumex crispus	Curled Dock
Rumex hydrolapathum	Water Dock
Sanguisorba officinalis	Great Burnet
Scutellaria galericulata	Skullcap
Saxifraga granulata	Meadow Saxifrage
Senecio aquaticus	Marsh Ragwort
Senecio jacobaea	Common Ragwort
Silaum silaus	Pepper-saxifrage
Sonchus asper	Prickly Sow-thistle
Sonchus oleraceus	Smooth Sow-thistle
Sonchus palustris	Marsh Sowthistle
Tanacetum flavum	Common Meadow Rue
Taraxacum officinale agg.	Dandelions
Taraxacum palustre	Little Marsh Dandelion
Thalictrum flavum	Common Meadow-rue
Tragopogon pratensis	Goat's-beard
Trifolium dubium	Lesser Trefoil
Trifolium pratense	Red Clover
Trifolium repens	White Clover
Trisetum flavescens	Yellow Oat-grass
Urtica dioica	Common Nettle
Veronica anagallis-aquatica	Blue Water-speedwell
Veronica beccabunga	Brooklime
Vicia cracca	Tufted Vetch

Species recorded in **Portholme Meadow**. Derived from an EN survey, 2003 by Sarah Lambert supplemented by records from Susan Smith, Brampton Rd. Huntingdon.

NOTES